THE
CLOSE TO HOME
30TH
ANNIVERSARY TREASURY

Other Close to Home books by John McPherson

THE
CLOSE TO HOME
30TH ANNIVERSARY
TREASURY

JOHN McPHERSON

Andrews McMeel
PUBLISHING®

Introduction

It has been quite an experience for me to compile this book and look back over 30 years of being a syndicated cartoonist. When I started cartooning in my mid-twenties, I had no idea I would be at it so long, and would still be having a great time with it all these years later.

In putting these cartoons together into one book, I sifted through my archives and looked for the cartoons that grabbed me the most. Readers might think that we cartoonists find everything that we draw as being funny. But, speaking for myself, I definitely have favorites! I tend to like the "edgier" cartoons, those that might be on the cusp of being shocking, though I never want to upset people with my work and ideally want to get them to laugh out loud. Cartoonists walk a fine line between being really funny, and being possibly "sick" with their humor. (I definitely lean toward the sick side.)

I think cartoons fall into two primary categories: those that are just funny because they are outrageous, and those that readers can really relate to as something that happens to them in their lives, and that relatability gets them laughing. To me, the latter are the ones that carry the most humor clout.

When it came to selecting cartoons, I turned to my family and asked them to go through and choose their favorites over the years, and it has been fun to see which cartoons struck them the most. Their selections account for about twenty percent of the cartoons in the book, and I really appreciate their insight. As a humorist we can get "too close" to our work and lose perspective on whether or not a cartoon truly is funny, so the frank opinions of friends and family can really be helpful.

Close To Home deals with family life, office, sports, travel, education, and parenting to name a few themes, but one theme clearly tops them all in sheer numbers, and that is healthcare. People often ask me why I do so many cartoons on doctors and hospitals, and the answer is quite simple. Where there is stress, there is humor, and nothing is more stressful than having our health on the line.

It may seem that I am making fun of being sick and laid up in the hospital. But what I am trying to do is get viewers to defuse a difficult situation in life by finding something funny hidden in its midst. Hopefully, I am able to get people to laugh at their plight and help lighten a moment that might otherwise be overwhelming.

Regardless of the themes, I hope you will enjoy the cartoons in the book. I had fun drawing them and hope you do the same in viewing them!

John McPherson
Spring 2024

"I made these out of leftovers from Thanksgiving dinner. They're gravy Popsicles."

"Sorry about the mix-up, Mr. Bixford. We'll be moving you to a semi-private room shortly."

"Uhh ... Excuse me, ma'am, but you've ... uh ... taken my cart by mistake. I believe that's yours there."

"Yeah, I know she shouldn't play with her food.
But that's pretty good!"

"Try jiggling the handle."

"Nah, it's still not quite right. Put in more worms."

"I can't believe you cleaned up your entire room
in five minutes."

	ONIONS	PEAS	CORN	BEANS	SPINACH
MIKE	HATES THEM	LIKES THEM	LIKES IT	HATES THEM	LIKES IT
TIM	LIKES THEM	HATES THEM	LOVES IT	HATES THEM	HATES IT
KATIE	LIKES THEM	HATES THEM	GAGS	GAGS	TOLERATES IT
LISA	Allergic	HATES THEM	Allerg.	Allerg.	HATES IT
WILLIE	THROWS THEM	TOLERATES THEM	THROWS IT	THROWS	THROWS

"And over here we have Tyler's 'Blue Period.'
Notice the strong, sweeping strokes that seem
to leap right off the canvas."

Budget wedding photos

9

"Don't be too impressed. It's not real. My kid made it out of Legos."

"How many times do I have to tell you kids to stop giving each other shocks? You're scuffing up my rug!"

"Mom, he is *not* a date! Danny and I are just friends."

"Why on earth can't you learn to pull up closer?!"

"Are you sure this is the honeymoon suite?"

"His high school reunion is tomorrow."

"The coffeemaker is broken."

"Maybe our price is too high."

"What am I doing? I'm making this
two-pronged outlet into a
three-pronged outlet."

"We're training him to go only
on the newspaper."

"I lost my whistle."

"I thought the family rental rate was too good to be true."

"Oh, for heaven's sake! It's Stan and Lois Murdock
from New Year's weekend!"

"Well, look on the bright side.
It's the only weed in the whole yard."

"No, that's not what I said. I said I made a New Year's resolution not to eat dinner in my underwear *when your mother is here.*"

"All right! All right! We can get a dishwasher!"

"Management says they're fed up with losing foul balls and homers to the fans."

"Nice break!"

With a typical wedding cake costing $300,
Ed and Linda opted for the more
economical wedding pizza.

"This new attachment I got makes ironing
shirts a piece of cake."

"How on earth could I have known that your coat
was caught on the door handle?"

"It can be very dangerous to suppress a hiccup."

The staff at Wilmont Obstetrics just couldn't resist
pulling the fake sonogram trick.

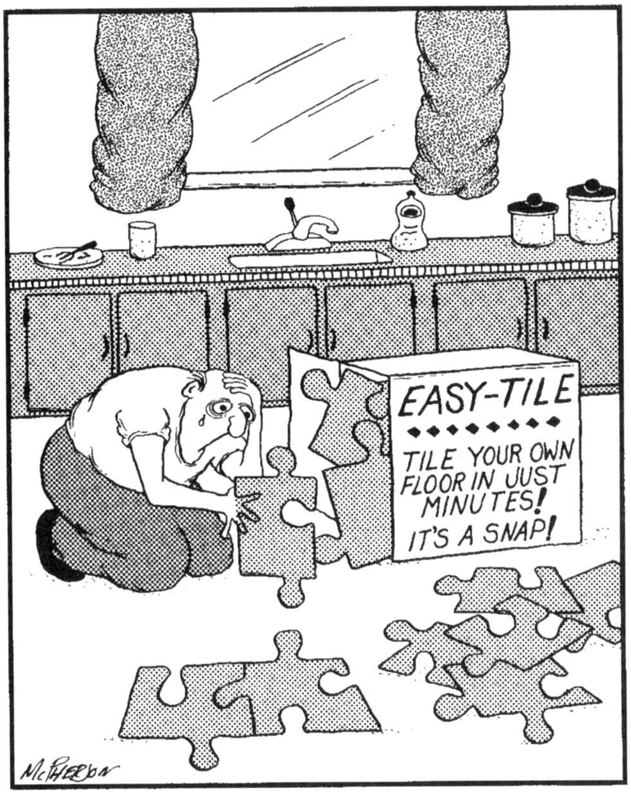
EASY-TILE
TILE YOUR OWN FLOOR IN JUST MINUTES!
IT'S A SNAP!

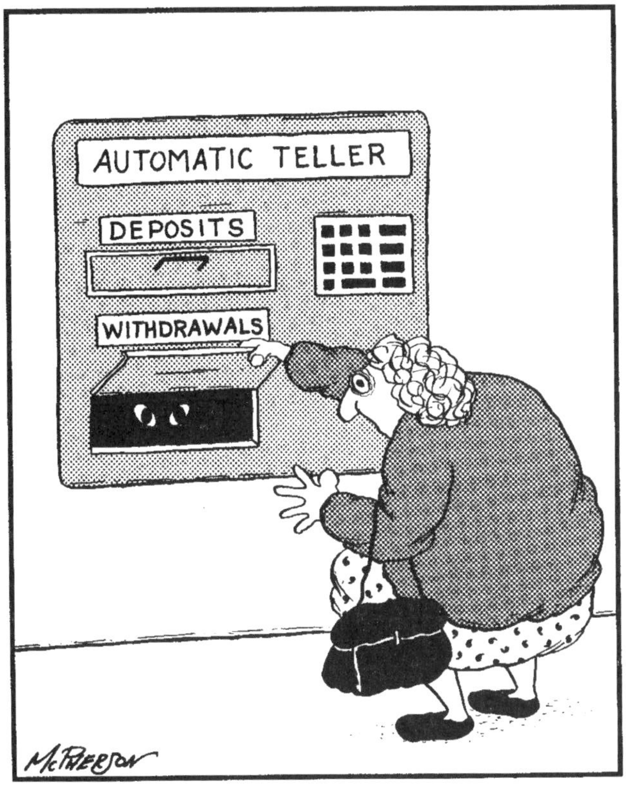
AUTOMATIC TELLER
DEPOSITS
WITHDRAWALS

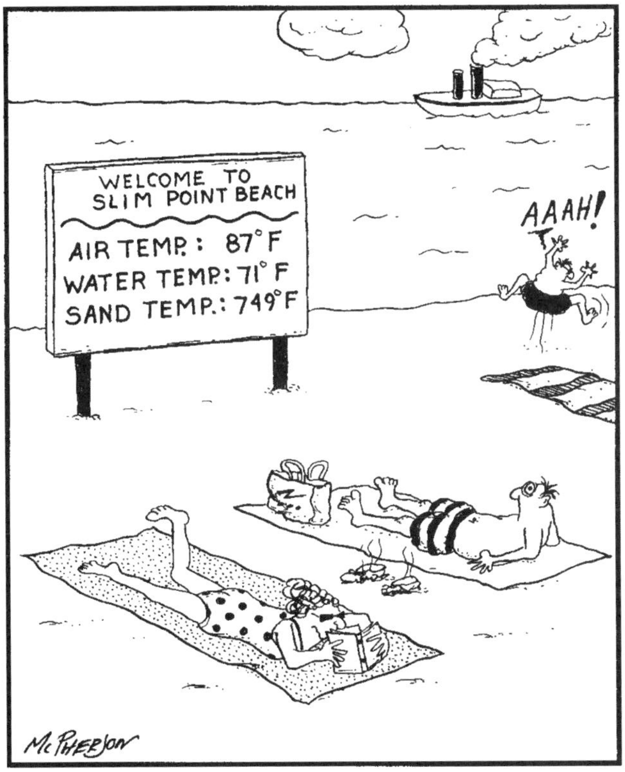
WELCOME TO SLIM POINT BEACH
AIR TEMP.: 87° F
WATER TEMP.: 71° F
SAND TEMP.: 749° F
AAAH!

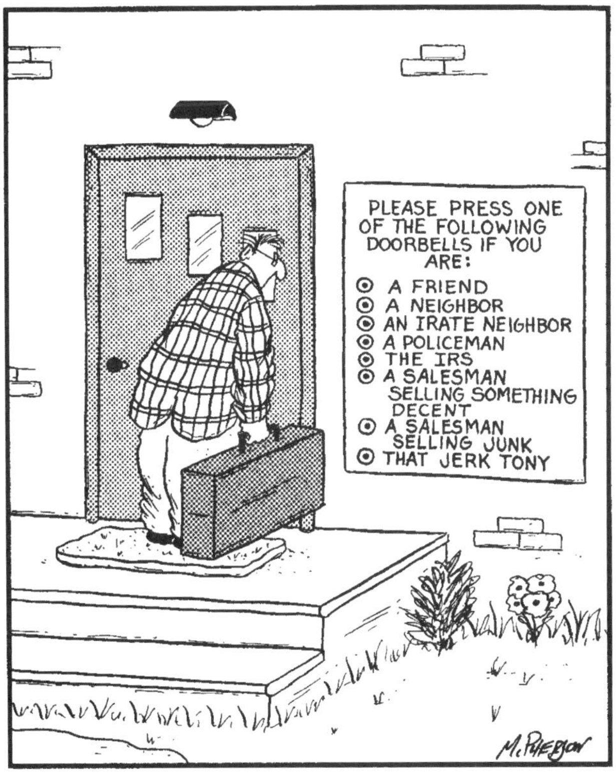
PLEASE PRESS ONE OF THE FOLLOWING DOORBELLS IF YOU ARE:
A FRIEND
A NEIGHBOR
AN IRATE NEIGHBOR
A POLICEMAN
THE IRS
A SALESMAN SELLING SOMETHING DECENT
A SALESMAN SELLING JUNK
THAT JERK TONY

"If you start to feel dizzy or weak,
get outside immediately. Your new
pacemaker is solar-powered."

No one ever messed with Wayne's car security
system, crude though it was.

"We don't know what those things are, but
everyone who has bought one says they're
very affectionate."

"Those are the new relaxed fit jeans."

"The intern who worked on me was an art major before going to med school."

"Mommy's having quiet time now, honey.
Go play with the other kids in the family room."

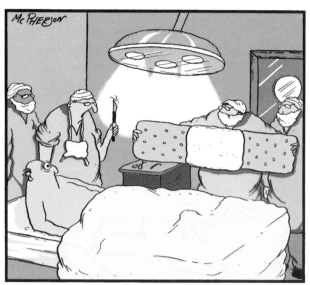

"Nurse Wright, when I give the signal, you slap that Band-Aid on him as fast as possible."

"It took some getting used to, but the kids love it. Plus, I don't have to vacuum anymore."

"Ya know, you're not exactly doing wonders for morale around here."

"Be careful. This plate is very hot."

"Here's 20 bucks. Let 'em keep riding until we get out of the movies."

"OK, hold perfectly still! We go with whatever name the baby kicks at!"

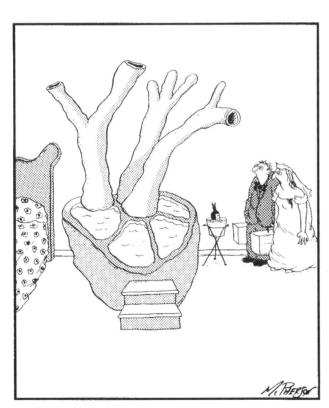

"This isn't the kind of heart-shaped Jacuzzi I had envisioned."

"The bad news is that Pepper is going to need a kidney transplant immediately. The good news is that, based upon our tests, you, Alan, are an ideal donor."

After losing the house to Al in the divorce settlement, Sheila used her gardening skills to carry out one final act of revenge.

Fortunately, an alert waiter spotted Danny's photo on the restaurant's blacklist.

"Which one of you found the fly in your soup?"

Jerry shows off his new central toilet paper system.

"For Pete's sake, slow down! This is that stretch
where there's always a speed trap!"

"Will you two knock it off with
the train sound effects?!"

"Jason! You apologize to Mr. Feffler this instant!
Or no pudding for you tonight, young man!"

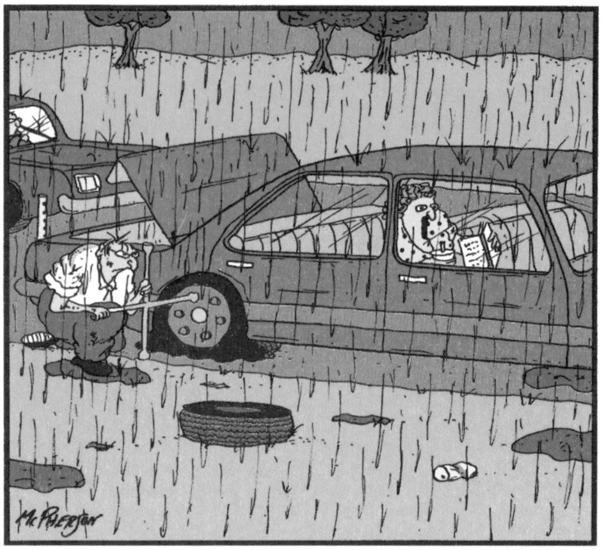
McPHERSON

"Ray! There's a bug in here!"

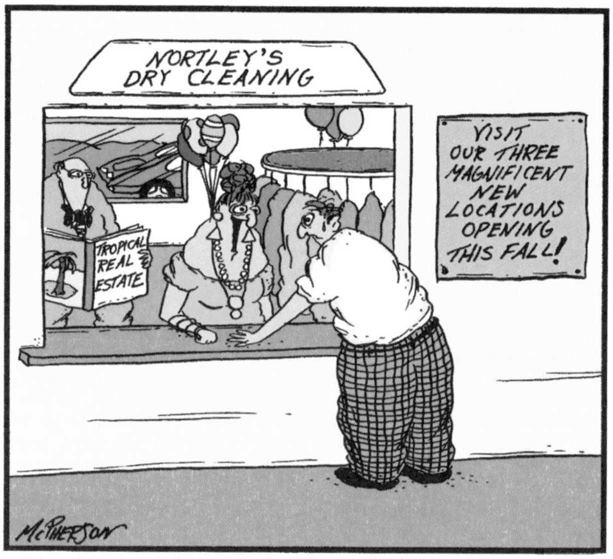
NORTLEY'S
DRY CLEANING
TROPICAL
REAL
ESTATE
VISIT
OUR THREE
MAGNIFICENT
NEW
LOCATIONS
OPENING
THIS FALL!
McPHERSON

"A winning lottery ticket? Gosh, I sure think we'd remember if we found something like that! Ha, ha!"

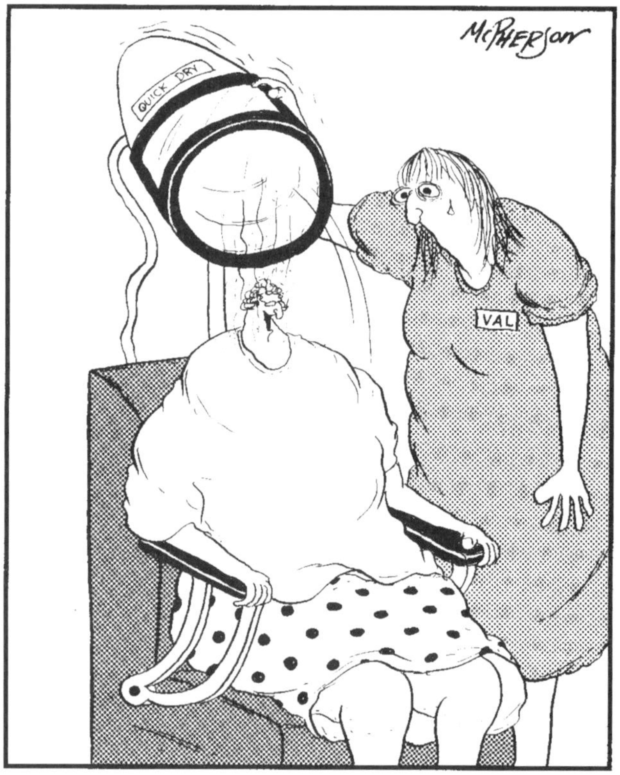
McPHERSON
QUICK DRY
VAL

"Wooo! Thank heavens! I was starting to think you'd forgotten about me!"

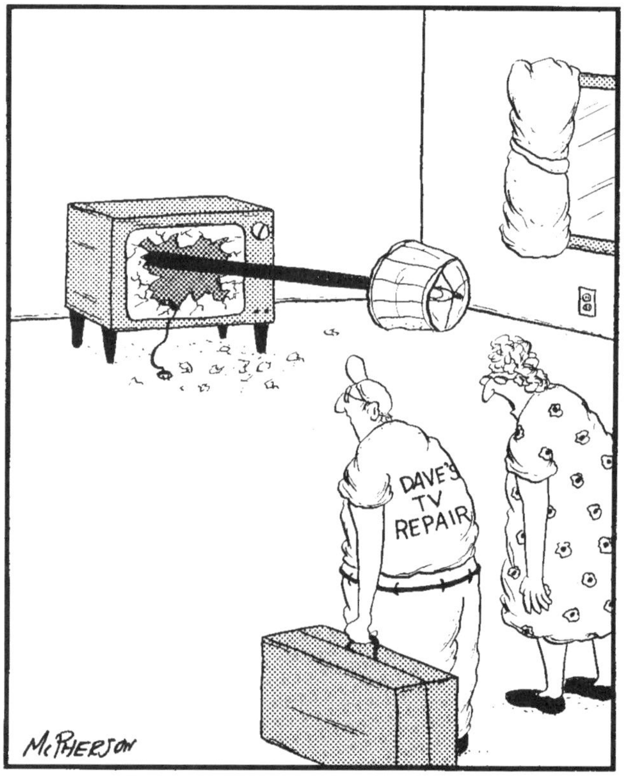
DAVE'S
TV
REPAIR
McPHERSON

"My husband said to send the bill to the New York Jets."

As Frank finished his six-hour shoveling job,
he suddenly heard the evil cry he'd heard
so many times before.

"George! Great news! I found my ring!
I didn't wash it down the sink after all!
It was on my dresser the whole time!"

"Mr. Stekson, we are very busy people.
Do you want the finest hair-replacement
procedure available or not?"

The Norstadts devise a subtle plan to force their newly returned adult son to move out.

"This'll just take a second. It was my husband's last request."

"Hey, Virgil, come here! Check out the cheesy-looking toupee collection El Dorko there is packing!"

The Gilmonts play a tension-filled game of chore poker.

"Anytime one of the kids gets an illness we cross it off. When we complete a row, Ed and I are going to Tahiti for three weeks."

At the Hair Center for Men research laboratory.

Evel Knievel at age 86.

Another marketing success for the Postal Service.

"Oh, come on. Don't be such a grouch! The kids worked so hard on it, and you'll be able to see where you're driving just fine."

"So then I said, 'A simple procedure that will give me better hearing than I've ever had, and without the hassle of a hearing aid?! Where do I sign?!'"

"Mr. Weingard, our contract with you guarantees to cure your baldness. At no point does it promise to regrow hair."

"Your prescription will be $80, or if you want, you can try our grab bag for $5 and hope you get lucky."

"The tile guy says he'll come back and replace the black tiles when our check clears."

At the Post-it Note research laboratory.

"Well, it figures! One more square and
I would've had bingo!"

Yellowstone park employee Reggie Nordell pulls the practical joke of a lifetime.

Bert's new Alaskan snow-shoveling hounds quickly became the talk of the neighborhood.

"OK, let's see... Myron Wuffle, president of one of America's largest HMOs. It says you're allowed in, but you can stay for only 24 hours."

Wayne Gretsky, age 10.

"I warned you not to ski so close to that snow gun!"

"And this is Dr. Sanborn. He's the one who will actually be performing your balloon angioplasty procedure."

"Hop in, Gail! This is all they had left."

"And for you, ma'am, the calamari."

Running late as usual, Todd slipped past his
manager's office in his new costume.

"Don't think you can weasel out of buying me a Jacuzzi this easily!"

"Who do you think you're fooling, Mr. Over-dramatic?! I know that backpack has a parachute in it!!"

M.C. Escher as a child.

Thanks to his new shark-attack simulator, Randy was able to have the entire beach to himself.

"I hate this hole."

"That suit is called 'The Optical Illusion.'"

"The bad news is we have no idea what's wrong with you. The good news is Ringling Brothers wants to hire you."

The school's new hall passes proved to be extremely effective in discouraging frivolous trips to the rest room.

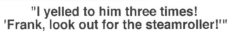

"I yelled to him three times!
'Frank, look out for the steamroller!'"

How to tell when you're on Santa's naughty list.

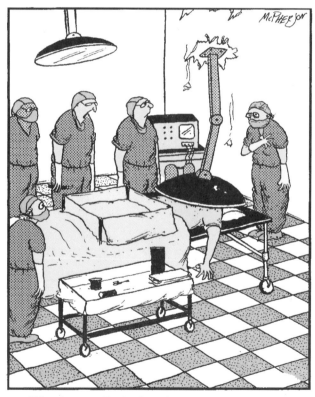

"Ten-to-one that when he comes to he tells one of those stories about seeing a bright light at the end of a tunnel."

"I told you it was a bad idea to stop
and get doughnuts first."

"It says: 'W-A-T-C-H ... Y-O-U-R ... S-T-E-P!'"

"Those morons down in 2-C had a skylight installed!"

"Bill! Don't forget! The vet wants samples!"

Disaster at the Rogaine® plant.

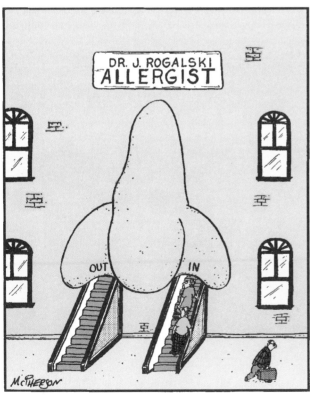

"You gotta admit, it does make it easy to find the place."

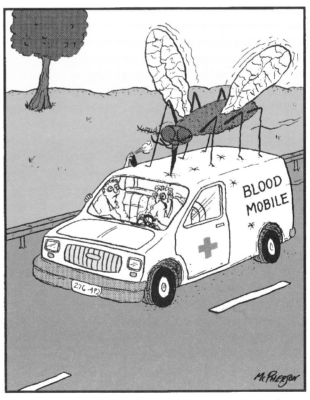

"Is it still there?!"

"We had her declawed, but we wanted to make sure she could still defend herself against other animals outdoors."

"Well, don't just stand there, Tommy! Open it up and see what's inside."

"Frank! It's Gloria. I need to know where you keep the keys to the riding lawn mower."

Renowned white-noise recording artist
Bobby Shamley.

"It's a PALM TREE, you IDIOT!!
A PALM TREE!!"

"This isn't what I had in mind when I
signed up for the pet therapy program."

At the United Construction Workers' College
2002 graduation ceremonies.

"Who did you say did your bypass surgery?"

"But that's the beauty of it, Rita! I don't have to
worry about my fat intake today. I'm having a
quadruple bypass tomorrow!"

"Thank heavens the plumber knows CPR!"

"Right now the baby is *not* in the proper position
for delivery, but I'm confident it will shift
in time for your due date."

"Say goodbye to our fly problem!"

"I'm gonna gather a little firewood, honey.
You go ahead and get some sleep."

"Really? You're allergic to apricots? Now that's
a shame. Yes sir, that is a shame."

"Everyone else is complaining because you're
the only one who has a window, so I've been
ordered to paint over it."

The horrifying secret behind duct tape.

"For heaven's sake, will you just give it up and admit that you need reading glasses!"

While rearranging Brandon's room during his freshman year in college, the Cranstons discover he'd been telling the truth all these years.

"Really, I'm serious. He's the guy who invented Styrofoam packing peanuts."

MILLVIEW CHIROPRACTIC ASSOCIATES

CRACK!...CRACK!... CRACK!...CRACK!

49

"Well? How did I do?"

"WAIT A SECOND! THIS ISN'T OUR DAD!"

"It powers the TV. I'm hoping he'll lose 10 pounds during the World Series alone."

"They say this is the closest Mars has been to Earth in 60,000 years."

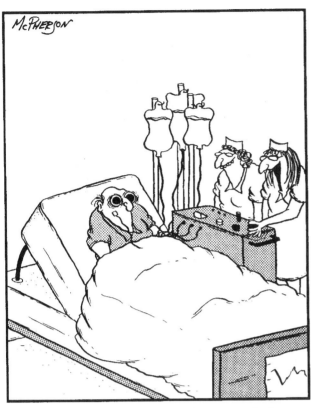

"Hey, Carol! Look how big his eyes get when you turn this blue dial *way* up!"

"Congratulations! You're going to have a disease named after you!"

"We ran out of IV bags."

"If you start to feel dizzy or weak, get outside immediately. Your new pacemaker is solar-powered."

The office erupts as veteran computer analyst Dave Valhoski makes his one-millionth mouse click.

"Don't worry, ma'am. I kept it good and warm for ya' underneath my shirt."

"And approximately how many balloons did he inhale as he was making the silly voices?"

"Dang! Looks like another job by the
Silly String Bandit!"

"I just wish he'd get a hobby or something.
He's been retired for a month now and he just
won't give me any space."

"I told you three times—put your car in neutral!"

At the Home for Little Kids Who Made a Face and It Stayed That Way.

Having tried for years to put some zest into their marriage, Carol finally turns Leon's head with her new Top Flite teddy.

"If you think this is bad, you should see his other car."

"Bummer. What are the odds you'd get up here and discover you're severely allergic to clouds?"

With 22 victims and the culprit never found, the Great Wedgie Attack of 2004 would go down in Weston High history.

"Here, I want you to do three laps around the maternity ward on this to see if we can speed up your labor."

The boys down at Witt Construction were having hours of fun with their new Nerf wrecking ball.

"No. 2, step forward and take three full swings."

"This new equipment is a godsend."

"Just relax, will ya? MapQuest says this shortcut will shave 17 minutes off our trip."

"It's classic Ambrose. He was always looking for ways to save a buck."

Ben and Jerry as kids.

"So . . . where do you see me in five years?"

"Those ones there? Those are eggnog cows, Robby."

Carol was the first member of her skeet-shooting team to get married.

"Roger, I think we need to talk about your trouble with intimacy."

At the National Whoopee Cushion Testing Facility.

Doug fights back at soaring gas prices.

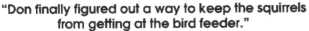

"Don finally figured out a way to keep the squirrels from getting at the bird feeder."

"This new guy is getting on my nerves."

"Oh for heaven's sake! Don't tell me the dog faked you out AGAIN!"

"Just stave them off! I'm putting for eagle!"

"So you ADMIT that labeling my client as 'naughty' is based upon hearsay from other children, not from any actual facts!"

"Oh, for heaven's sake! We had him declawed, but he's still destroying the furniture as much as ever!"

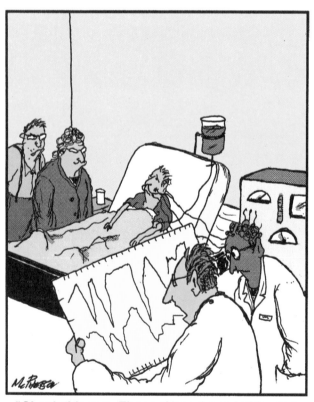

"Check this out. These sharp drops in his vital signs coincide with visits from his in-laws."

"Would you folks care for some fresh maple syrup on your pancakes?"

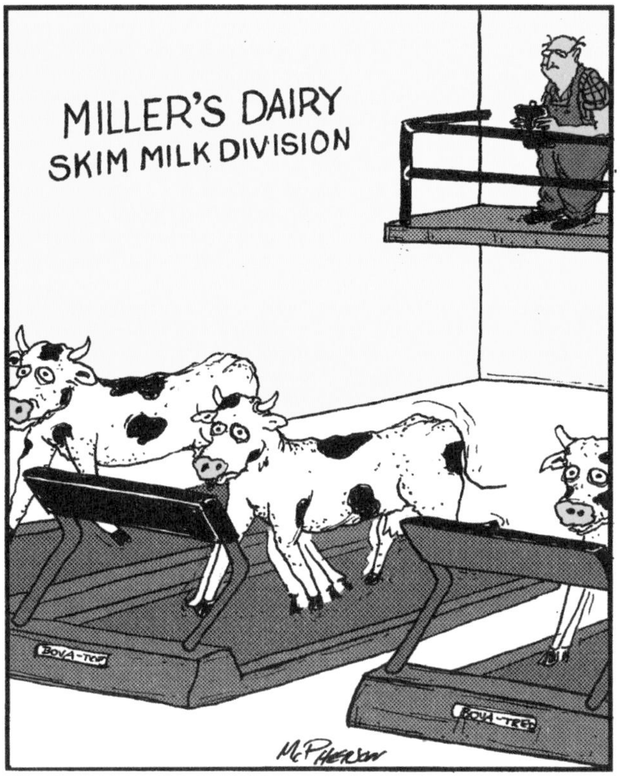
MILLER'S DAIRY
SKIM MILK DIVISION
McPHERSON

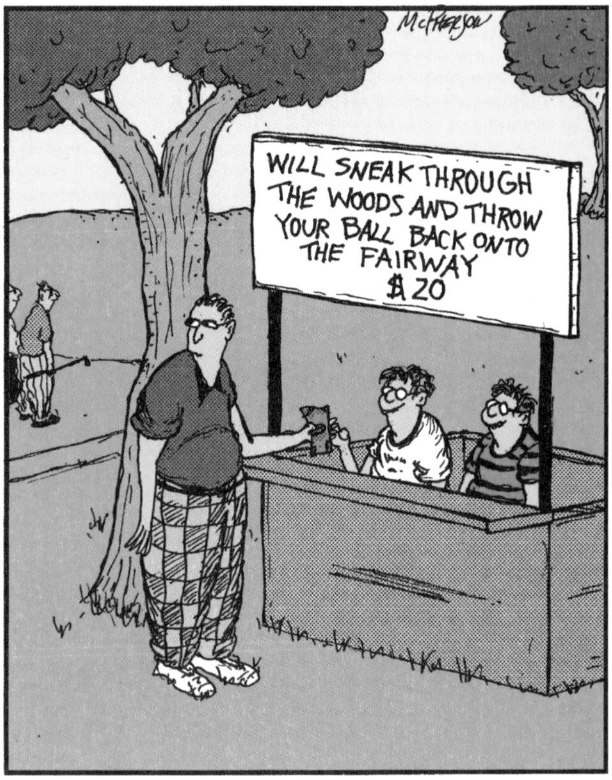
McPHERSON
WILL SNEAK THROUGH THE WOODS AND THROW YOUR BALL BACK ONTO THE FAIRWAY
$20

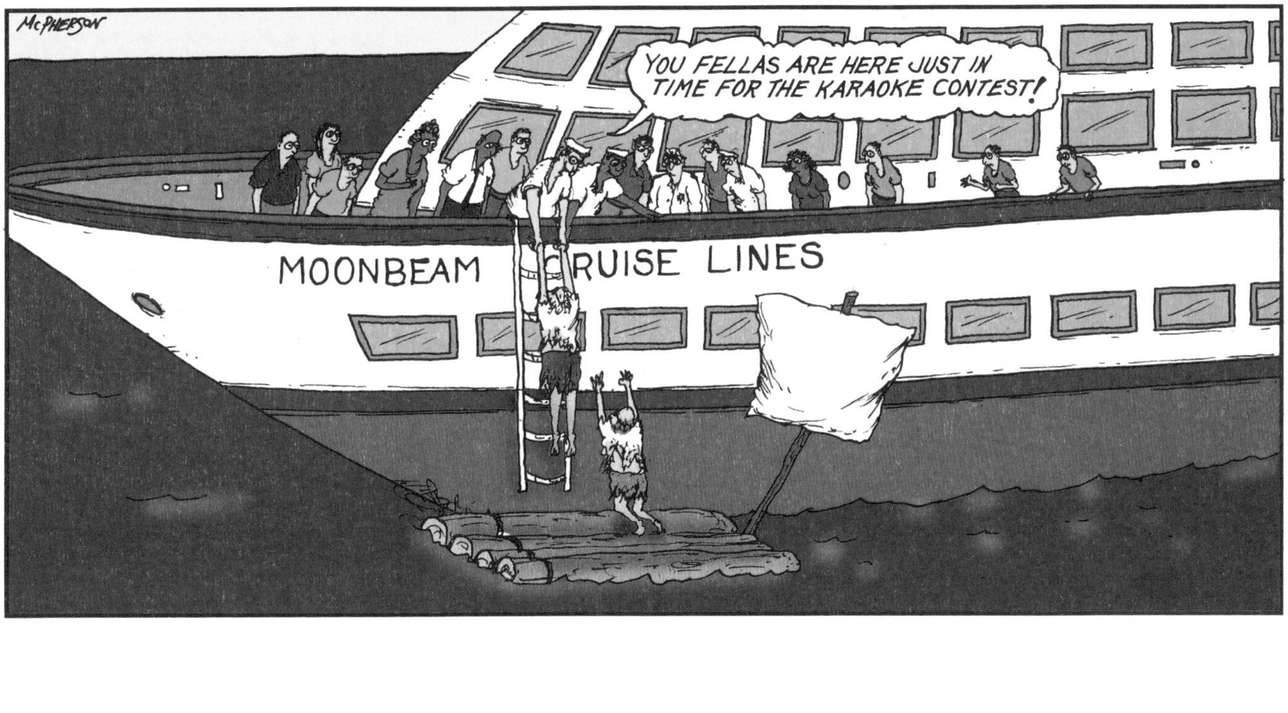
McPHERSON
YOU FELLAS ARE HERE JUST IN TIME FOR THE KARAOKE CONTEST!
MOONBEAM CRUISE LINES

An amateur magician as well as an obstetrician, Dr. Kingsley felt it was important to bring some humor into the delivery room.

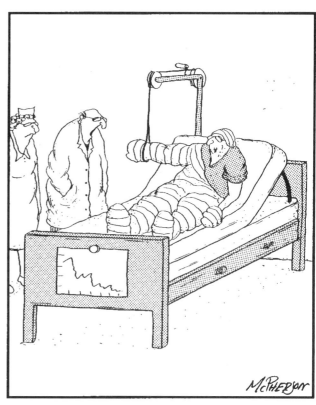

"Your insurance company is refusing to pay your medical bills due to a pre-existing condition. It says you were already an idiot before you decided to Rollerblade down the interstate."

"The doctor says it's just a pinched nerve."

"Go ahead and tee off. Then I want you to listen to this wheezing."

To prepare for Halloween night, the Milner brothers trained with 20-pound trick-or-treat bags.

To discourage him from jumping on the bed, Ryan's parents covered his ceiling with flypaper.

I THINK IT'S TIME WE TELL KEVIN THE TRUTH ABOUT SANTA CLAUS.

"For an extra $25 we can set
the surgical lamps on tanning mode."

"I know that he's a cardiologist, but it still
gives me the creeps."

"Hold it RIGHT there, buster! Nobody leaves
the floor before signing out first!"

"Look at those dang fool teenagers, wearin'
their pants hangin' down low
like a coupla idiots!"

Entry-level tech-support jobs.

God creates the cry of a baby.

"The Bosmans' wedding announcement?
Stick it on the fridge so we
don't forget about it."

"I'm afraid I can't allow you on the plane, sir. Your hair is too sharp."

Early birthday parties.

"Stu and I joined the Adopt-A-Highway program."

As Jason was learning to walk, the Grunsleys made sure he was outfitted with roll bars.

"Our house is directly in the migratory path of Canada geese, so we keep the windows open until mid-November."

"You idiot! This isn't what I told you to buy!"

The unsuccessful predecessor of Silly Putty™.

"Before you're released, would you mind taking our exit survey?"

"I don't CARE how many times we have to circle the building! I'm not turning the car in until we've used up all the gas I paid for!"

While driving north on I-80, the Gilfords are thrilled to have a rare sighting of a superdelegate.

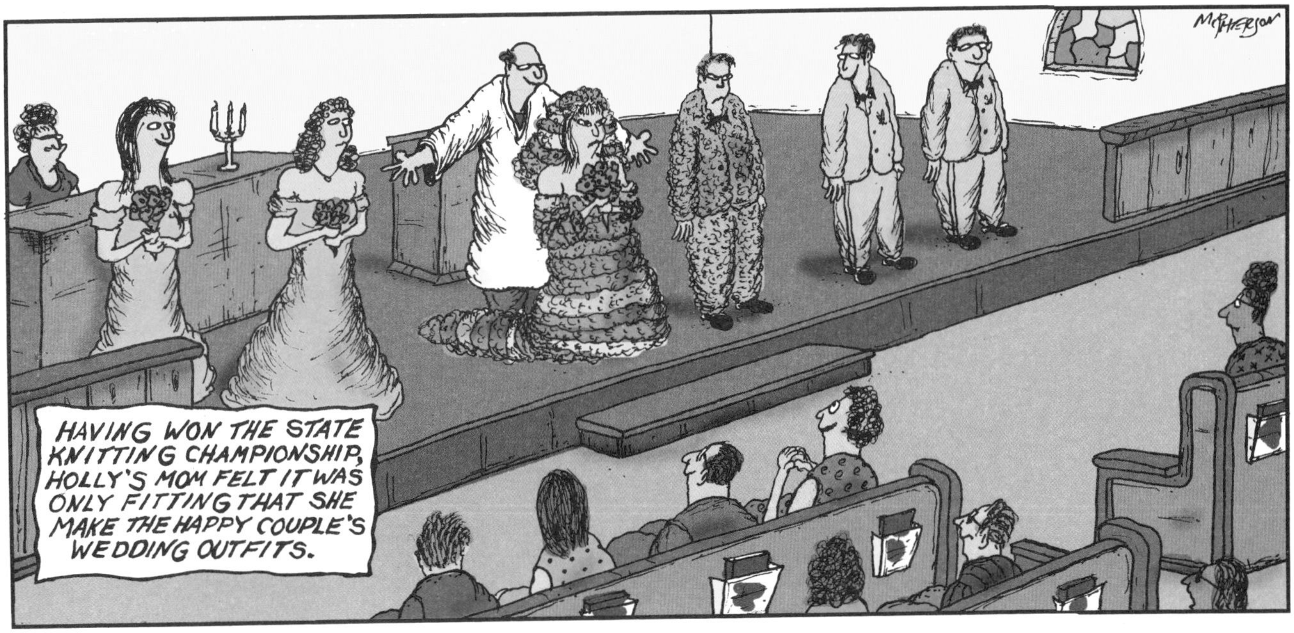
McPHERSON
HAVING WON THE STATE KNITTING CHAMPIONSHIP, HOLLY'S MOM FELT IT WAS ONLY FITTING THAT SHE MAKE THE HAPPY COUPLE'S WEDDING OUTFITS.

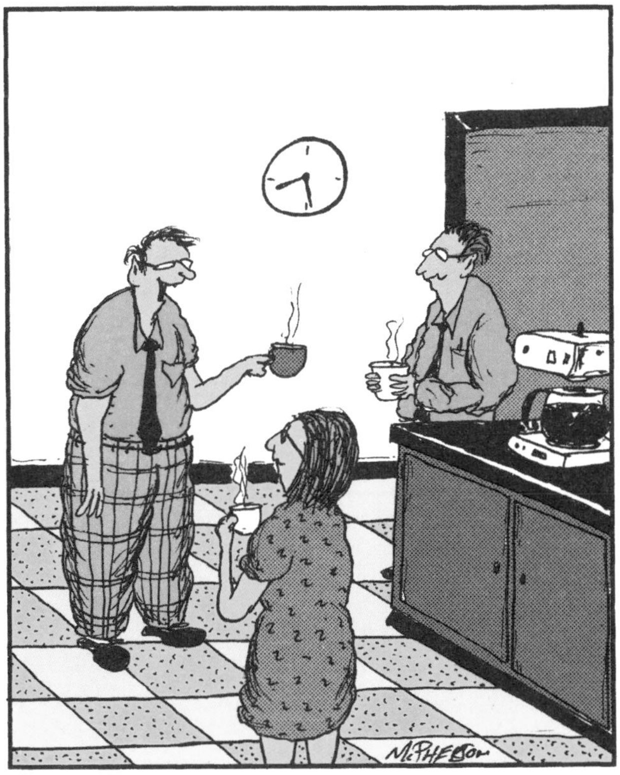
McPHERSON

"I worked out a deal with management that if I trim two minutes off of every coffee break, they'll let me retire 14 months early."

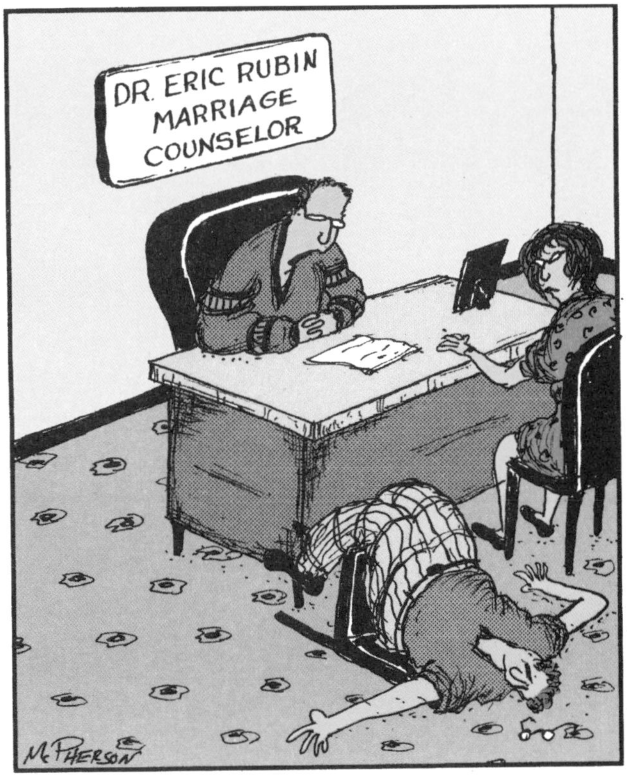
DR. ERIC RUBIN
MARRIAGE
COUNSELOR
McPHERSON

"That's precisely what we are talking about, Bob. You cannot simply play dead anytime Vera raises a difficult issue."

Early shopping lists.

"You're just more affected by Novocain than most people, Mr. Cromley. You should regain full use of your legs in a day or two."

76

"I couldn't figure out how to get rid of those stupid subtitles, so I slapped duct tape over them."

"I'm trying to live a greener lifestyle. I'm using only organic eggs from free-range chickens."

"It's a new strain—chicken noodle pox."

"Whatsa matter?! You got lard in your ears, fathead?! I TOLD YOU, I'm lookin' for the book 'How to Win Friends and Influence People'!"

Thanks to an elaborate system of mirrors, every employee at Vecon Industries had a window view.

WILL YOU RELAX? HE'LL NEVER NOTICE, PLUS IT'LL SAVE US A TON IN GAS.

"Everyone ... ah, ha, ha! ... get out of here!
We've got a ... ha, ha ... leak in our ... hee! ..
laughing-gas tank! Oooo-weee! Ha, ha!
Go on, you scamps! Shoo!"

"Didn't anybody tell you? Fridays are
casual day in the O.R."

"Joyce, write this down in Mr. Cutler's file: 'thump ...
thump-thump ... thumpety-thump ... boink.'"

"We're conducting a study on the healing power of
humor. As Boppy performs for you, let us know the
precise moment that you feel the kidney stone pass."

"I have no idea what's going on here, but
I suggest we all do as he says and
get into the mudroom closet."

Tired of constantly sending her money, Jill's
parents installed an ATM in her dorm room.

Howie unwittingly gets up on the wrong side
of the bed.

Josh tests his theory that by driving backward
through a quick-pass toll lane, he can
get money ADDED to his credit card account.

"What a RIP-off!"

As a world limbo champion, Dave could make it to an airplane's restroom, even when the beverage cart was in the aisle.

While no one was looking, Wanda placed a decal with her name on it on the Hollywood Walk of Fame.

"That'll teach your mom to stop giving us obnoxious parenting advice. I slipped the dog's electric Invisible Fence collar into her back pocket."

"How the heck could we lose
a $14,000 pacemaker?!"

"Well, what'd you expect?! I've been telling you
for two years that we need health insurance!"

"We don't have to anesthetize patients anymore. I just walk in with this and they pass out in a second."

The game of LIFE™, updated edition.

"I think you'll get a kick out of our 'haunted' MRI, Mrs. Hanratty."

"Steve! Watch out! Runway models!"

"Warren, come take a look at this virus
I found in the patient's blood sample!"

"Watch this. We put a Bluetooth on the dog's
ear so we can call him from miles away."

"DIBS ON HOWIE'S SANDWICH!"

Having dumped the bag of ashes on the table, Stew hid behind the door and waited for the X-ray technician's reaction.

"Yep, that's right. Just the one bag for the five of us."

To his dismay, Dave's GPS system gets stuck on the Scooby-Doo voice setting.

"How do you feel about Alternative Medicine?"

"I'm looking forward to flying this airline because they boast about having more leg room than any other."

"I hate it when Bill brings work home."

"You can have our standard treatment for $150 or, for just $25, you can hug this cactus as hard as possible."

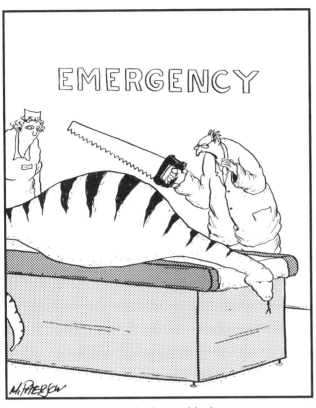

"OK, Mrs. Morris. I need to have you scoot as far to your left as possible."

"I gotta find a new HMO."

Advanced parenting techniques

"Well, I'm sorry, but if you don't have a receipt for the pacemaker there's not much we can do for you."

"I tell ya, that was sheer genius getting those flimsy chairs for the waiting area! We've been selling a ton of diet pills."

"That's just a warning to lay off the cream-filled doughnuts and start getting some exercise."

"Can I interest you in one of our frequent-buyer discount cards?"

An avid soccer player, Roy head-bumps his playing partner's ball in for a birdie.

Milt had a friend video all of his dates so he could see where he screwed up.

A talented ventriloquist and impersonator, Greg Melvin gave the deceased's family and friends a touching farewell.

"Yeah, I hear the squealing noise too. Probably just a bad wheel bearing."

"Ray, I think you may have a winning lottery ticket in the pants you were buried in. I need to have you read off the numbers so we can verify it."

"At $50 a sandwich board per week, multiplied by 800 students, it'll really help balance the school budget this year."

"Nobody showed up because they could all foretell what was going to happen."

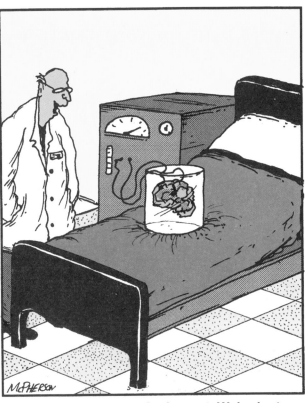

"All your vital signs look great. We're just waiting for a donor body now."

"It's Happy Hour in the courtroom, so instead of the eight years of jail time you should be getting, I'm cutting it down to four."

The course's new, half-eaten, fake golfer helped it to rake in hundreds of balls a week from the pond.

"The Maynards aren't practicing the rumba after all. Turns out there's a wasp's nest on their back porch."

"I've kept it on there for seven years now. Never had a speeding ticket."

"Did I mention the comment I made at last night's school board meeting?"

"Gloria, I would appreciate it if you would stop greeting the patients with 'Welcome to the Crack House!'"

Wes Lunker uses a visual aid to enhance his report on the solar system.

The annual Christmas bonus check wind chamber is always a big hit at Kelpman Industries.

Unfortunately, Lyle had already sent nasty e-mails to his boss, three vice-presidents and the CEO.

"The building is designed so that every employee will have a view."

"Perfect! They went for the peanut butter! OK, now for phase three. Slowly walk to the window and dive into the swimming pool!"

"I have to do this favor for my dad. It's just a 25-minute drive, a quick drop-off, and then we can head to the movies."

"I got a new lawn-mowing app for my cell phone."

"Those are all highway miles. The previous owner was a pharmaceutical sales rep."

The new Teen Driver Bungee: Keeps your teen within a three-mile radius of home!

The latest in bandage technology.

"That's one of our new carts for dieters."

"Starting a vegetable garden has been a great way for Greg to relax and really get in touch with himself."

"I know you're worried about Tibby, Mrs. Lutz, but we simply don't allow people to stay overnight with their pets."

"This way, I make sure I don't have more than five cups of coffee."

Hoping to increase her chances of passing her driver's exam, Jen rented a nun costume.

To prevent aisles from getting plugged up, Food Baron outfitted its carts with shopper prods.

"For heaven's sake, Alan! Get the skimmer!"

"So den, weez tie on t'ree cinderblocks, and ... BADA-BING! ... Down to da bottom he goes! And dat was da last time anybody saw Bennie Da Mole!"

While entertaining some clients, the surgical glove lost inside Tom during his bypass surgery makes an untimely reappearance.

As he settled into the chair in the principal's office, Brian quickly noticed the desperate scratch marks made by previous visitors.

New in household safety:
Nerf™ stairways.

"Football season never really ends, Hon.
It just goes into remission."

"The kids are trying to power the entire house with their potato project."

"I hate how my legs stick to the car seats when it's hot like this, so I use PAM cooking spray on them."

"YES! There it is, people! I have just detected my ten-thousandth piercing!"

Barry's friends and co-workers at the morgue give him the mother of all surprise parties.

Chuck found an ingenious way to make some extra cash on the weekends.

"Man, I hate it when they want to water-ski!"

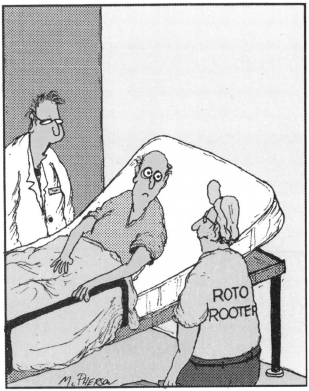

"The plaque buildup in your arteries is getting severe, so I've brought in a specialist."

"No, no, no, you idiots! The blindfold goes on him! Put the blindfold on him!"

"These budget cuts stink."

"He rigged this up to make sure that his kids would visit his grave."

Ed could tell that the new secretary was not working out when he found her using Wite-Out to get rid of spam e-mails.

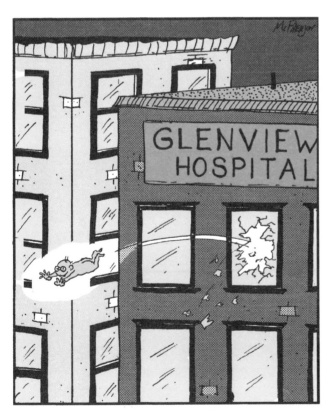

The astounding birth of Eddie the Human Cannonball.

"Things are pretty backed up today, so we'd like you to take each other's blood pressure, weight and temperature."

"Of all the low-down, dirty, rotten tricks!
I figured I was 210 yards away, so I hit
my five wood!"

"Trust me. Nothing beats these new
micro-greenhouses when it comes to growing hair."

Told by his golf instructor to "be the ball,"
Ron visualizes his upcoming putt.

New for seniors: all-terrain walkers.

"Check it out. The defibrillator paddles are great for making paninis!"

"You folks missed a heck of a sale!"

"Your new pacemaker comes with 50 million free beats! You can buy additional beats at pulsemore.com."

"THIS is actually the original portion of the house. The other rooms were added in 1974."

"Dave is very apprehensive about his colonoscopy tomorrow."

"You know, I just feel like somewhere along the line we have failed as parents."

Roy wanted to dazzle his blind date with his sparklingly bright smile.

"When I ran the numbers, this was WAY cheaper than buying new carpeting."

"This remote is for the TV, this handles the cable box, that one the stereo, and this one is for the robot that brings back all the remotes."

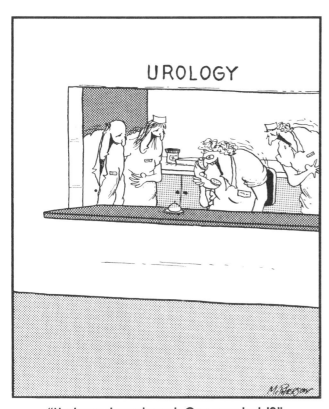

"Urology department. Can you hold?"

"For 35 cents, would you like the extended warranty on the Life Savers? It covers theft, loss, dropping in the dirt, choking..."

In a bold shift, the IRS begins setting up roadblock audits.

"Hey, cut me some slack! It was pitch black out when I landed us here!"

"Just for the heck of it, I totaled up all the grocery coupons that you ignored in your entire life and they came to $112,489!"

At the National Junior High Backpack
Lifting Competition.

At the Dernco Hard Hats quality-testing
facility.

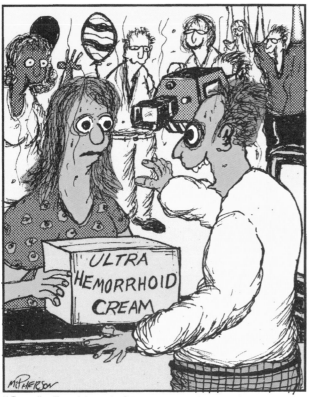

"Carrie Beckley, YOU are our ONE-MILLIONTH customer! Wave to your friends, fans and admirers around the world!"

"Pssst! ... Hi, we're the grandparents of this little fellow, and for $500, we're wondering if you would change his name from Tyler to David."

"Wow, yeah...um, that is some, uh...really bad shredding. Ummm...our new guy, Chip, did that. I'll get him out here to...um... talk to you."

Little-known Oscar categories.

Vinny "The Mole" was a firm believer in
Take Your Daughter to Work Day.

Pork futures.

For the sake of convenience, many dog and cat
owners are turning to the new pet-mounted stain
removal systems.

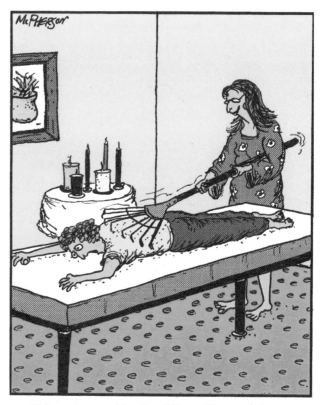

"I have to say I had a different impression
of what Reiki is all about."

"Whoa! I hit the jackpot over here, Gary!
How are you doing? Getting anything good
in those drains over there?"

"OK, deal! If you can fix the fuel pump,
we'll take $500 off your ambulance fee,
but hurry it up!"

To make the Kindle seem more booklike,
the latest version includes a paper cut option.

"Oh, too bad. I think you are IDEAL, but the
cards say that you are NOT going to get the
sales rep job here at Vision Quest Tarot Cards."

"I'm sorry, sir, but this flight is very
crowded. So to save space, we are binding
each passenger with bungee cords."

"The plumber said it was either this or
I had to give up chili nachos forever."

"Him? He created the 'Man Bun.'"

"Hey, hon, have you seen my tube of
pumpkin spice hemorrhoid cream?"

"OK, everybody just caaaalm down! Now, I'm gonna lower your guy into the water and you come and spit Vern back into the boat."

"Good news, Mr. Fillbert. There's been a computer error. You're up here six days early, so we're sending you back down."

Badly in need of a restroom and with no rest stops for the next 82 miles, Holly makes a desperate move.

"OK, OK! Your allowance goes to $15 a week and you can stay up until midnight on weekends! Now get me out of here!"

"The defendant, owner of Chompo Hot Dog Buns, INTENTIONALLY sells buns in bags of 8, despite the fact that hot dogs are sold in packages of 10!"

"So, including this and messing up my parallel parking, how many points do I have off my exam so far?"

A steamy new book sends shockwaves through America's farming communities.

"Will you just relax and forget about whether or not you left the coffeemaker on?!"

"Oh, him? That's Frank. My parents made me take in a boarder to cover the cost of my car insurance."

"Well, technically, visitation hours were over 15 minutes ago. But I think the healing power of good friends is too amazing to be denied!"

"Ooh! Ooh! I just got the Wordle in two guesses!"

"I'm much happier since I quit my job at the paint store, but I no longer dream in color."

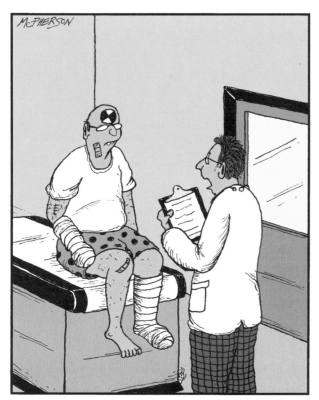

"You know, I can't help but wonder if the birthmark on your forehead has something to do with your tendency to be so accident-prone."

"You have done an amazing job! So good, in fact, that you are all being fired and replaced by the PZ-1200!"

The Kellers' new Memory-Foam™ mattress confirmed Barry's suspicion that Sheila was having an affair with the mailman.

"You boys will be happy to know that this bread is 100% gluten-free!"

From the makers of Silly String comes Rowdy Rope.

An obscure xylophone player for most of his life, Stan Lugivial was launched into stardom with his hugely popular iPhone ringtone.

"Hey, Dan, did you see a duodenum come scooting under the door here...oh, phew! There it is."

"Well, this explains why your check engine light has been on."

"They're just wax, but they keep my daughters' boyfriends from getting the least bit out of line."

"Uh, Viper? You're going to hate us for this, but we need to go back and get our toothbrushes."

"Eddie, it's a nice touch, but it's really not necessary to put a mint on their pillows."

"I ran the numbers and it turned out to be $180 cheaper to send Uncle Leon this way versus cargo."

"Hold it! IRS. I want 35% of every dime you just stole plus 15% self-employment tax!"

"Brad, your mother and I never got around to saving for your college education. Here are 100 instant lottery tickets that we hope will make it up to you."

"With the new water restrictions, we had to start slathering the Slip 'N Slide with Crisco."

"Just for fun, I like to show folks the number of bugs they mistakenly swallowed throughout their lifetime."

"When we ran the numbers on the cost of an electric paper shredder, getting a goat turned out to be way cheaper."

"Since you all have bad head colds and you can't taste anything anyway, we're having some really ancient leftovers."

"We do all of our diaper changes using computer-guided drones."

At the National Skeet Shooting Institute's 2013 graduation ceremony.

"THIS STINKS! Baseball-sized hail!"

"I'd bang a 5-iron off the Hancock Building, up 37th St., off that garbage truck, and you just MIGHT get back onto the fairway."

"Frank had claustrophobia all his life."

"In all fairness, you never covered 'Bridge out' signs in class."

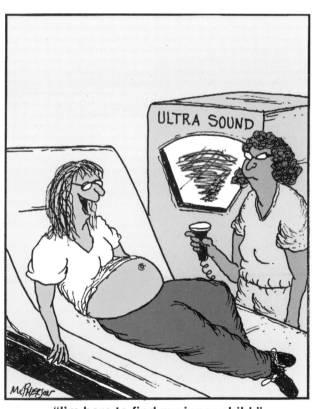

"I'm here to find my inner child."

"Ok, let's see here ... Gina Vurkle ... WHOA!
THREE unpaid parking tickets?! No getting
in here until those are cleared up!"

"Norm felt guilty about having Muffin declawed, so he signed him up for karate lessons."

"Didn't you hear the new safety mandate? Pitchforks have to be sanitized before we can stab anyone with them."

"For added realism this model has roadkill every eight feet."

"Me? Whoa, hold on! There is a guy next door who smokes and is 35 pounds overweight. Another neighbor swears at his dog..."

"Tiffy doesn't believe in capital punishment."

"And this one I got for coming in first in the sack race at the base picnic."

While getting some things in the basement, Monique is visited by the Ghost of Christmas Turkeys Past.

"Why am I not surprised?"

With her stove out of propane, Eve was forced to use the kids' Easy Bake Oven to prepare dinner for her 12 guests.

"After about 14 days of Elephant Therapy, Mr. Derbler, you should start to feel some improvement in your memory!"

"Ohhhh. LOVER boy. I thought the 'o' was an 'i'! Well, too late now."

"No, not in a circle, you idiots!! Get in a straight line, with the prisoner against that wall!"

Wayne's new Bubble Wrap shirt made him an instant babe magnet.

Chemistry teacher Vera Schwantz introduces her new scratch-and-sniff periodic table.

As part of their study on the Crusades,
Mr. Wagley's social studies class invades
fourth period algebra.

"The whole surgical team worked really hard
on him, but we reached a point where it was
really gross-looking, so we quit."

"I have a lot of great people in my life, but
when it comes to loyalty, no one compares
to my four-legged friends."

"We gave up on getting our daughter to clean her room, so we just laid linoleum over all the junk."

"This is the final quality control station for the Men's Hair Club."

THE FROZEN TONGUE DEAD LIFT.

CHICKEN FIGHTS ON ICE.

THE 50-METER SALMON SWIM.

REJECTED WINTER OLYMPIC SPORTS.

"I just thought he was taking an awfully long
time to line up his putt! He's dead!"

Outfielder Kirby Wilnut sold a signed
baseball for $1,500 rather than make the
play at home.

How they make marshmallow fluff.

"Kevin and Kim, this is my husband, Armand. Armand was a security guard at the Leaning Tower of Pisa for 22 years."

"Honey! Kevin just texted his first word!"

Soccer games took on a whole new meaning
for the parents of Hillsdale Youth Soccer.

"The kids just get so upset when a pet dies,
so we decided to get one of these
tortoises that live to be 150."

"Hey, Tony, get over here quick if you want to
see a seagull's face magnified 100 times!"

"I figured out that I can save six cents per roll of
dental floss if I buy the unwaxed
and wax it myself!"

A former Olympic high jump star, Bert arranged a little surprise for his bride as they entered the honeymoon suite.

"No, it's not a script. It's a letter from my son, who is in med school, and I'm wondering if you can decipher his handwriting."

"I hate the greenskeeper at this course."

A common caveman nightmare.

Fish revenge.

Drew and Paul loved nothing better than
a day spent bodysurfing.

To cut costs on in-flight movies, Comet Airlines had its pilots circle a drive-in for an hour and a half.

"When we looked at the cost of a hotel, camping, an RV...these new fiberglass people shells just made a lot more sense."

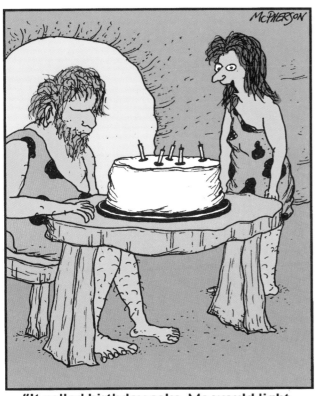

"It called birthday cake. Me would light candles, but fire not discovered yet."

"It's 'Take Your Daughter to Work' day."

"You have the right to remain silent. Anything you say or do can and will appear online in every corner of the world..."

"Again, I ask the prosecution to stop badgering the witness!"

"All right! $13,600 more from another Final Jeopardy!"

"I can give you 25 new warts for $700, but if you want hairs growing out of them, it will be another $500."

"Oh, for heaven's sake! This is the third drone trick-or-treater we have had tonight."

"I'm just tossing these Nerf lightning bolts at people who have committed minor screwups."

Patrons who successfully bobbed for lobsters at Rinaldi's Restaurant got fifty percent off their dinners.

Tea strainers for mobsters.

Where croutons come from.

Once a month, Barb sold off all
the items that her kids' buddies
left at her house.

Oliver Twist goes camping.

"We just want to make sure you're getting
plenty of fish oil in your system."

"Great Scott, Ingrey, it's
the Ottoman Empire!"

**How humans will evolve due to
the incessant taking of selfies.**

**"That's in case we need to make
a water landing."**

144

Though she did not know it, Carol began to suffer from visible thought bubbles.

"We're running a bit behind, so I'm going to take whichever of you screams in agony the loudest."

"So there's a cardinal at the feeder. Big deal. If I've seen one cardinal, I've seen a hundred of 'em."

"We sort of think we changed your oil,
but we're not sure."

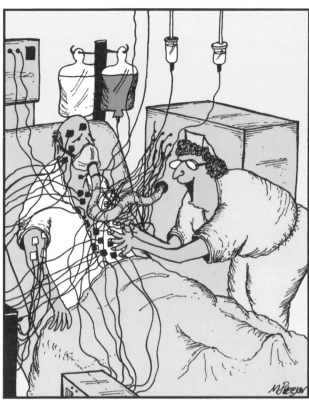

"Sorry to be a nuisance, but I think my phone
charger got mixed up in here somehow."

RUBIK'S CUBICLE

With over 800 students in the senior class, Ferdstein High installed a zip line to speed up the graduation process.

Primitive weed eaters.

Google Earth: The early days.

"He invented the hula hoop."

"We send a 250 million dollar satellite 300,000 miles into space and you idiots left the lens cap on it?!"

The first pyramid scheme.

"MOM! It's me, Zoey, from 35 years in the future! I'm 42 now and people think I'm 60! Slather me every day with SPF 30!"

"Me always carry extra in case
of breakdown."

149

OB-GYN Kenobi

"Your honor, the defense rests."

"I tell ya, work has gotten to be so much more fun since we hung that rubber spider in there."

The summer home of the
Old Woman Who Lived in a Shoe.

At the funeral of 1932 bobsled
gold medalist Hans Voortman.

"Pssst! Look what I snuck past those
bonebrains!"

Foolishly, Aunt Gert hit the turbo button
on the new stair lift.

"Eat up! These things are loaded with iron!"

151

Recognizing the next bungee jumper as the bully who gave him a massive wedgie in 9th grade, Dan exacted his revenge.

Oscar and Squiggy stumble onto an illegal pulled pork operation.

"He was electrocuted while smoking an e-cigarette in the rain."

The truth about the Venus de Milo.

Cindy was careful to make sure she was
getting a bargain on toilet paper.

"Wow! Upside-down cake!
My favorite!"

"Give me a few minutes. I'm doing a little
work on the side for Gertman's market."

"To help you quit smoking, I've put one
exploding cigarette in each pack."

"It's the latest in undercover police vehicles. I bet you were pretty surprised to see a cow bearing down on you at 85 mph, eh?!"

To make sure that her kids got proper nutrition, Sandy relied on the new Veggie Patches™.

"You can scoff all you want, but by sweeping up the birdseed at weddings, I've saved us over $180 in the last 25 years!"

"Isn't this just the greatest?! Color-Your-Own wallpaper kits! I have this great geometric pattern for the den, a Mayan pattern for the ..."

"No, you IDIOT! CAESAR! Like the Roman emperor! CAESAR!! ..."

"Somehow we just didn't raise him right. The kid is drafting in his Fantasy Neurosurgeon League."

"And this is my husband, Vern. He'll be our appetizer tonight, and Dave Albright over there will be our main course."

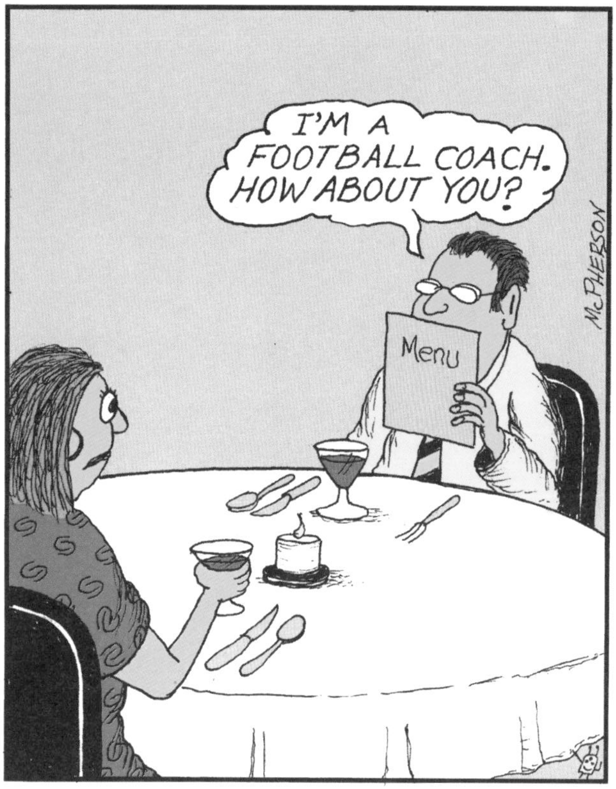
I'M A FOOTBALL COACH. HOW ABOUT YOU?
Menu
McPHERSON

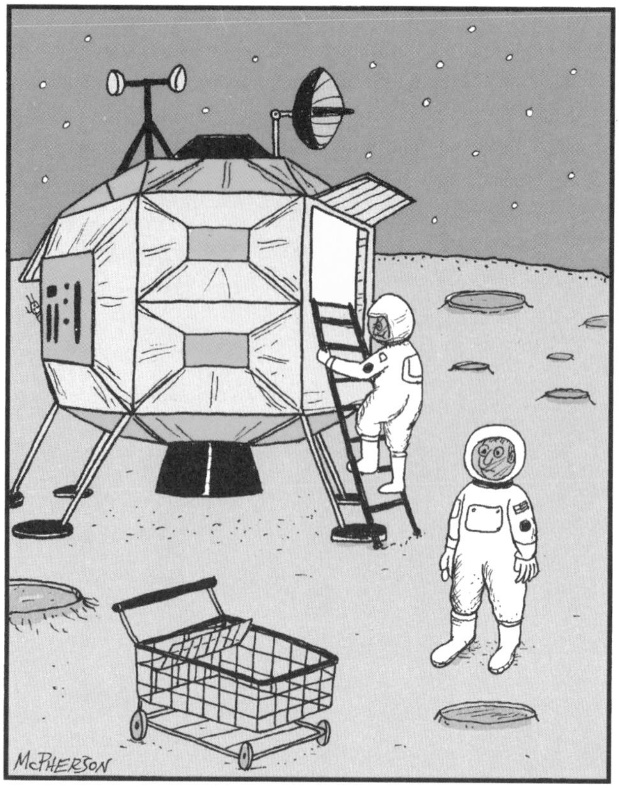
McPHERSON

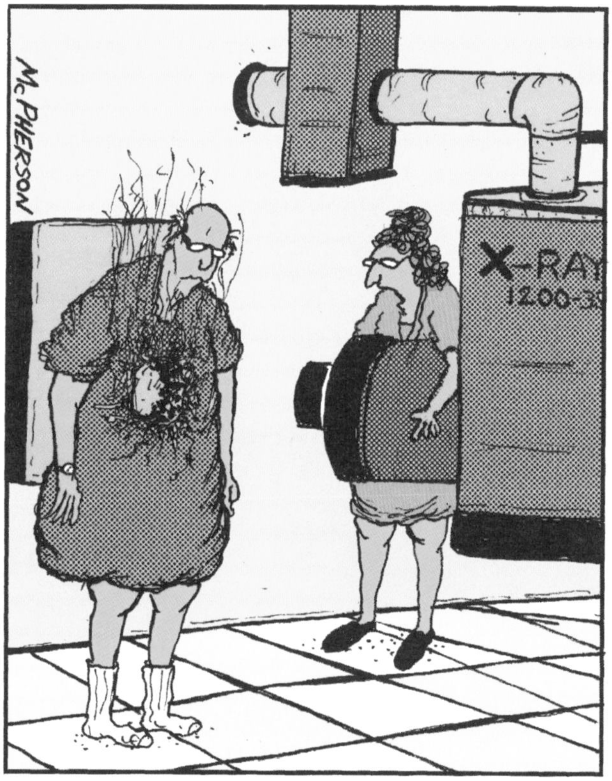
McPHERSON

"Whoopsee."

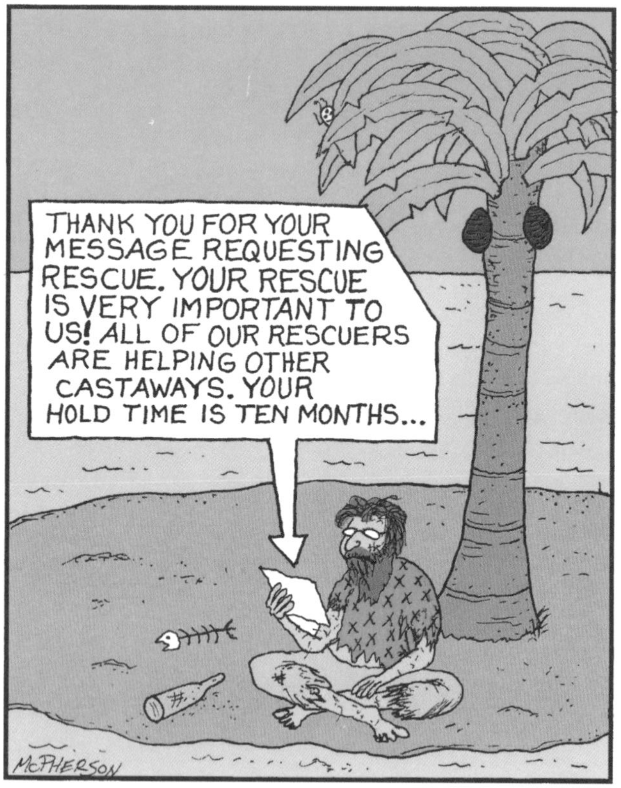
THANK YOU FOR YOUR MESSAGE REQUESTING RESCUE. YOUR RESCUE IS VERY IMPORTANT TO US! ALL OF OUR RESCUERS ARE HELPING OTHER CASTAWAYS. YOUR HOLD TIME IS TEN MONTHS...
McPHERSON

"Yes! We've done it! Created the first answering service that makes it impossible for a caller to reach an actual human being!"

"The advertising paid for all of the burial costs."

"So that's it?! All they have is SACKS?!"

"What the?... Our driverless car was nailed for going 75 in a 45 mph zone and we owe the city of Elmira $120!"

Despite the controversy, this new pipeline would save thousands of trips and over four tons of reindeer food a year.

After adding the drive-up window, the Hillsdale Day Care experienced a 30 percent increase in enrollment.

Just as she was giving her Airbnb guests a tour, Shirley discovered that the kids had created an "amusement" ride for their pet rats.

Wanting to impress the pirates right up to his last moments, Sawbuck executed a perfect one-and-a-half gainer.

"She's watching WAY too much TV these days!"

"Unbelievable! They're looking for those Pokemon things!"

"All RIGHT! According to my Fitbit, I've burned 457 calories just since the battle started!"

"So, as I walk away, the magnet on my belt attracts the metal plate on the toilet and automatically puts the lid down!"

Suspecting that her performance review
might not go well, Hannah made
sure to bring three cans of Silly String.

"The pills I gave you will clear up your reflux,
but for your lower GI problems and your
knee pain, you need to see a veterinarian."

"I'm not disputing the fact that geocaching
is a great family activity. I just wish you
hadn't put one of the caches in our bedroom!"

"On the plus side, we don't have to
worry about burning our feet on the sand
anymore."

"This is just until I've saved up enough to buy a dishwasher."

"Could you show just an OUNCE of compassion?! A show that your mother's been binge-watching for nine days just ended!"

"Bob, your yelling is exactly what he wants. My new parenting book says he is just testing our authority and we should ignore him."

Annoying social trend number 121: Cutesy restroom symbols that no one can understand.

"Mom, I have three stomachaches."

"I forgot to mention: Warren is on that new Plankton Diet!"

"So, you can live a short time and feel great, or live a long time but feel lousy."

"Oh, that's Slade. The state gives us $800 a month to house him here and it helps them with prison overcrowding!"

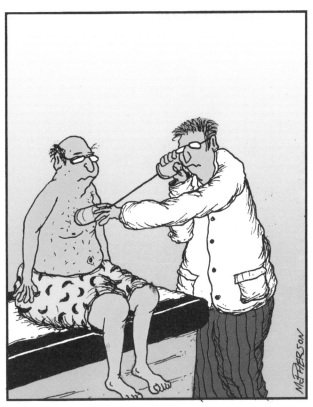

Budget Stethoscope.

Though they hoped to improve their passenger approval ratings, Phoenix Airways goofed by adding restroom attendants.

"You did great at most of the nanny tryout stages, especially 'Bottle Feeding' and 'Bedtime.' But you blew the 'Refusing to Allow Bikers to Party' stage."

"Yeah, right, Dad! Dad says that not long ago, kids used to CARVE jack-o'-lanterns out of REAL pumpkins!"

"Ha! Here's a funny little tidbit! You spent a total of 223 days and 17 hours trying to remember passwords to miscellaneous websites!"

"Nuts! Mrs. Ratzer, will you call one of the third grade classrooms and get some kids to install this new operating system for me?"

"Dang! If only we could determine the time of death. Right down to the minute. We really need to know the EXACT minute!"

"Isn't that great? The city is lacing the water supply with a light pumpkin spice flavor!"

"Zarsky, I don't know how you did it, but you dropped enough pounds to wrestle in the lightweight division!"

Brindini's Law of Inverse Proportional Leftover Containers: The smaller the amount of food, the larger the container will be.

"This is AWFUL, Higgins! This could lengthen people's lives by years and destroy us!"

"Great news! I found the warranty, and it's totally replaceable!"

"Have you ever considered the possibility that your feelings of inadequacy may be affected by the birthmark on your forehead?"

While hiking deep in the mountains, Gary and Brenda found the answer to a centuries-old question.

"Isn't that great? All pacemakers now come with an outlet for phone charging."

"So we took a wrong turn! Now that we're here we might as well see if we can set a new record!"

"Up above you can see the infamous debt ceiling, folks."

"Relax. I'm just here for your houseplants."

"I'm sorry, but my husband always sleeps nude."

169

"I TOLD you it was a stupid idea
to bring the termites along!"

Johnny Appleseed's later years.

"I'm rebranding myself as the 'Grin Reaper.'"

"OK. There's your new driver's license photo. The fee is $65 for your license and for $50, we WON'T post your photo on Facebook."

"You still want us to change the oil?"

"It's STILL not long enough! You need to tell ONE MORE lie, Pinocchio!"

"While you were away at college, Kyle, your father and I got inspired and transformed your room into a beekeeping colony!"

"I'm sure it is VERY scary, hon. But if you could just stand ALL the way up in his mouth, we will get MILLIONS more hits online!"

"Well, here's the problem, Wilbur! The seat wasn't in its full upright position!"

MODERN YOGA POSES

"PARKED TOO FAR FROM THE DRIVE-UP ATM" POSE.

"KILL THE ANNOYING MOSQUITO AT 3am" LUNGE.

"DISPOSING OF FOUR WEEKS OF PUTRID CAT LITTER" POSITION.

"My name is Santa, and I
ate 4 million, 243 thousand and
11 cookies in one night."

"Duncan, that is BRILLIANT! We can make a FORTUNE
by selling the mummy's wrapping as toilet paper!"

"Think of it! No more searching for
stench-filled restrooms! Now you can just keep on
driving and driving..."

"Calm down, Mrs. Horrigan! It's me,
Dr. Carpenter. We are low on masks, so
we've had to improvise."

"So, Mom, I got a 27 out of 50 on the
fractions test. That's like about a 90, right?"

Rather than getting dressed up for online business meetings, Jen relied on her new "Zoom Facade."

"Hey, Annette! Put this on! He should be coming to any minute!"

"WHAT THE?... WHAT KIND OF A TWISTED MIND WOULD DO SUCH A CRUEL THING?!"

"Frankly, this is a piece of cake for me. I was a substitute teacher at a junior high for 22 years."

To hold students' attention, many teachers are relying on iPhone costumes.

"The world's oldest mayfly died today at the age of 28 hours and 2 minutes! That story at 11, for those of you who are still alive."

Rapunzel gets a perm.

"Maybe our crust is too flaky."

"We got a device called 'Sani-TV'! As soon as it senses a disturbing news story, it switches to puppies playing."

"We've put bars on all your windows, hidden cameras all over, motion detectors, the alarm system ... there's NO WAY your adult kids can move home!"

"So, Heather, if you are NOT home by midnight, this video of your dad will be sent to ALL of your Facebook contacts at 12:01!"

"Aaaaahhh! Make it stop! I'll talk! I'll tell you where the money is!! Just stop that awful noise!"

"It's unbelievable. My wife ordered them from Vermont for $25, and the kids haven't turned on the TV since!"

Reindeer Games.

While eager to get their son Nate home from his first semester of college, the Sealys took no chances on getting COVID.

In a laboratory somewhere in North America, circa 1984.

"As you may know, I was voted president of the senior class, so I pardoned all of us who were in detention!"

"For heaven's sake! The city really needs to take care of these potholes!"

"How long have you had this mayonnaise? The expiration date is in Roman numerals."

"Our bank account password requires a number, a special character, two Swahili adverbs, a Greek letter, two state birds and a chemical suffix."

"It's great that so many places are offering vaccinations now."

"I bet you if we play our cards right, we can get a free dessert out of this!"

"Objection, Your Honor! This witness is a total surprise to us!"

Dr. Seuss dines out.

"This week's Special Person is Ed Smerd, who invented automatic water faucets that never work no matter how much you move your hands around!"

Scientists have discovered that men lack the gene that allows one to fold fitted sheets.

Few people know that Picasso started out
as a police sketch artist.

"Like many businesses, we're short-staffed.
We'll take $15 off your bill if you will
wash your dishes."

For votes that are totally deadlocked, Congress settles the tie with a bout of Rock 'Em, Sock 'Em Robots.

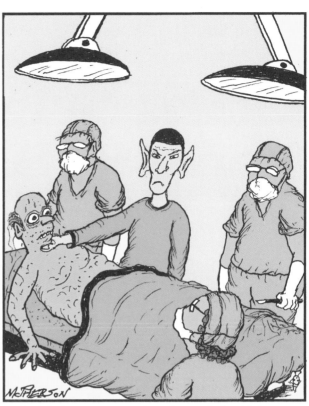

In his later years, Spock used the Vulcan nerve pinch to forge a successful career as an anesthesiologist.

In an ironic twist of fate, Rip Van Winkle and Sleeping Beauty end up on an online date together.

"Still having hot flashes, I see."

"I said to her: 'Velma, you're a witch! You work at NIGHT! A solar-powered broom won't cut it!'..."

Geek tattoos.

"I told you it was useless to trick-or-treat at the cable guy's house!"

"It's bad enough that they trashed the place and robbed us, but they also gave us a lousy Airbnb review!"

The NFL finds a new way to settle tied games.

"For cryin' out loud, I'm just delivering from Grubhub!"

"I'm from around here, but Todd actually grew up on Easter Island."

"The flypaper floors are a nuisance, but it's the only way we can retain employees."

"They're refusing to work out until we get a Peloton."

An early sign of fall.

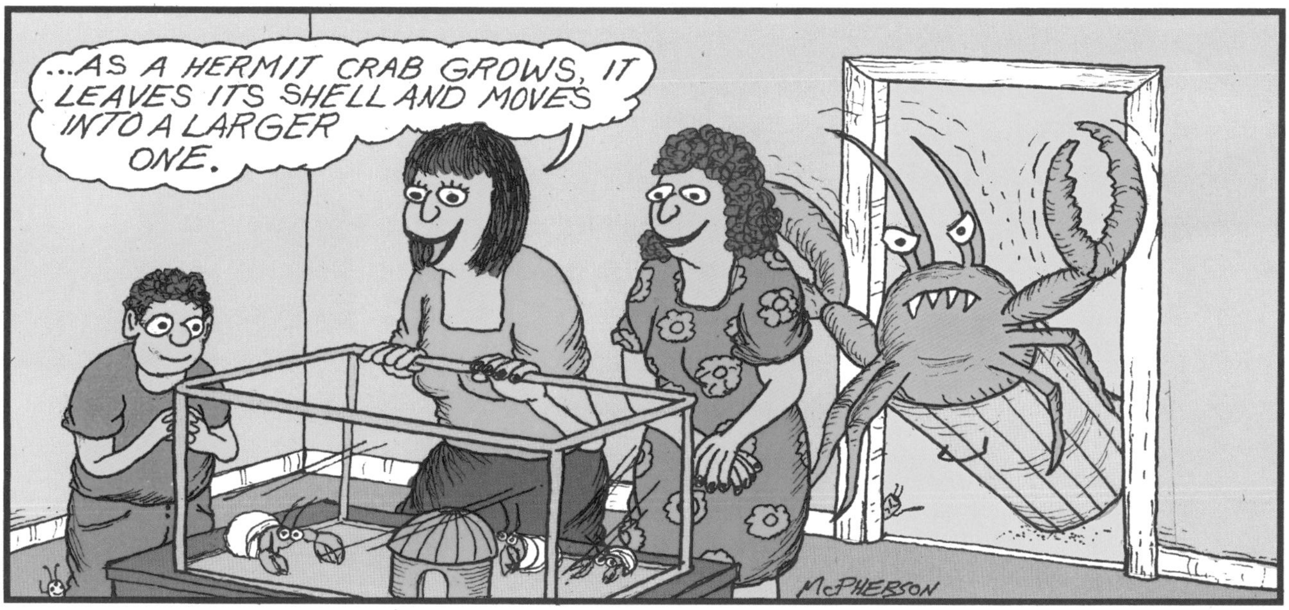
...AS A HERMIT CRAB GROWS, IT LEAVES ITS SHELL AND MOVES INTO A LARGER ONE.
McPHERSON

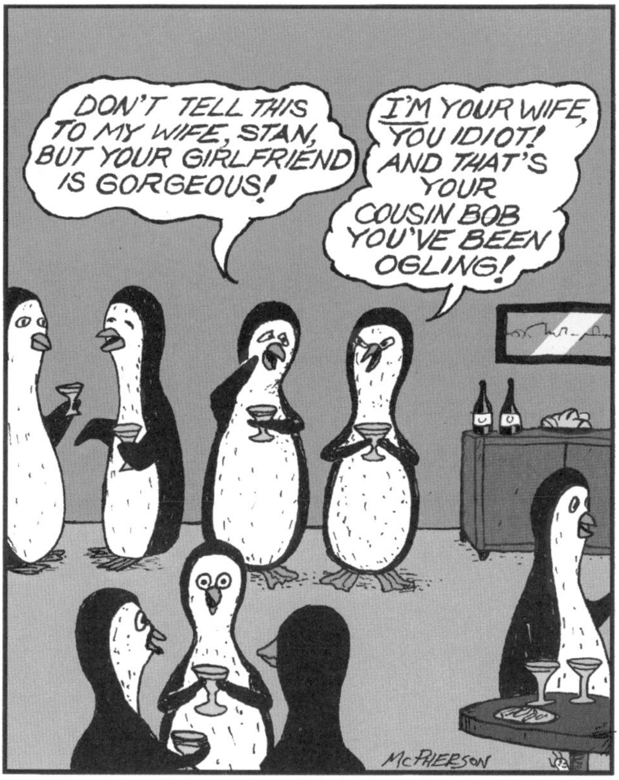
DON'T TELL THIS TO MY WIFE, STAN, BUT YOUR GIRLFRIEND IS GORGEOUS!
I'M YOUR WIFE, YOU IDIOT! AND THAT'S YOUR COUSIN BOB YOU'VE BEEN OGLING!
McPHERSON

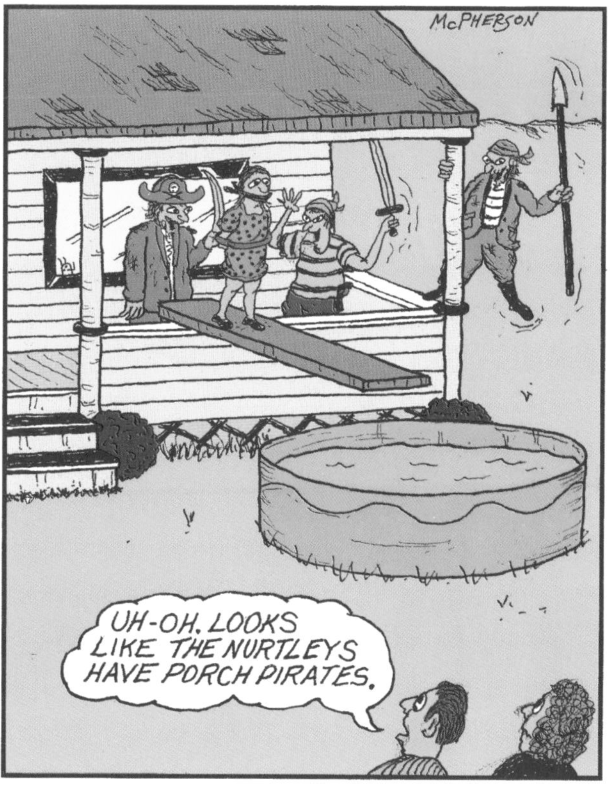
McPHERSON
UH-OH. LOOKS LIKE THE NURTLEYS HAVE PORCH PIRATES.

A FOOLHARDY SNOWMAN ACTIVITY.

Eel parties.

"Hey, you idiots! Knock off the pickleball and get over here and defibrillate this guy!"

"Brad is slowly transitioning back to the office in the wake of the pandemic."

These are two of my earliest drawings. They are pretty crude and each one took me forever to draw. But it was exciting to have something on paper that I could look at and feel like I was a cartoonist on some level. Like most cartoonists, my style has evolved greatly since my early years. That's part of the fun and the process.

"MEALS ON WHEELS."

"Well, yes Stuart, I suppose that's one way to spell it."

Ideas

When things are really going my way, cartoon ideas will just pop into my head—while I'm driving, out to dinner, in the shower, while I'm getting a speeding ticket . . .

But most of the time I have to consciously try to come up with them. To get cartoon ideas, I try to really focus on something in particular. If I just sit there going "funny idea . . . funny idea . . ." I get nothing. So I try to really home in on something—maybe an angry guy at an airport ticket counter, an airplane filled with crying babies, a doctor who hates the sight of blood. I try to think of mixing things that just don't go together or situations that will cause stress, because I know that if I can put my characters in a stressful situation, something funny is not far behind. Hospital settings are great sources of stress, which is one reason I do so many medical cartoons. I'm not trying to make fun of people who are sick, rather, I'm trying to bring some humor into an upsetting predicament.

Often, I'll sift through magazines to help spark an idea. Photos can really trigger some goofy thoughts. And goofy thoughts are the key to good cartoons, I think.

But sometimes I can sift through a pile of stuff and still come up dry. When that happens, I just sit at my drawing table and draw some bizarre scene and then see if I can come up with captions to make sense of it. It's a pretty effective way to break through a block and has generated some pretty funny cartoons. (Well, at least my mom said they were funny.)

Here are some examples of that method at work.

I drew this sketch of some movers staring at a huge hole in the floor. There must be one hundred funny things that one of them could be saying here. So here are four that I came up with:

1. "Man, they sure do build those Steinways great. That thing was in perfect tune right until it hit the fourth floor."
2. "For an elderly couple, they sure scrambled out of the way quickly."
3. "I say we bring in that big oriental rug next."
4. "I can't believe that nun down on the seventh floor actually tried to catch it!"

Now, not all of these are necessarily hilarious captions. I just sort of start writing. But the third and fourth ones work pretty well, I think. At this stage, I'll fax the cartoon over to my editor in Kansas City and he and I will try to decide which captions work best. He might even poll some other editors. And I might wander around a mall and stop perfect strangers to get their opinions. In this case, we liked the image of a nun trying to catch some large object that was hurtling at her. However, when I've shown this cartoon during speaking engagements, the crowd pleaser is always the oriental rug caption. Just goes to show you what my editor and I know.

Here's a great calamitous scene. A surgical lamp has fallen onto the patient's face.

1. "Cancel the anesthesiologist."
2. "Well, looks like Mr. Gardner is going to get his money's worth out of this nose job!"
3. "Ten to one that when he's recovering tomorrow, he tells one of those stories about seeing a bright light at the end of a tunnel!"

The first two are decent, but the clear winner is number three, and that's what we decided on.

Here I drew a snake in an emergency room with a large lump that obviously contains a person. I stared at it for a while and then decided that it would be funnier if the doctor was holding a saw. Endless possibilities, and just a funny image in itself.

Here are four captions for it.

1. "Before we resort to surgery, Mrs. Sanders, I'd like you to try 'Open Sesame.'"
2. "It's not that simple, Mrs. Sanders. This snake is an endangered species."
3. "Everything's going to be fine, Mrs. Sanders. We've given the snake a laxative and you should be out of there in four hours."
4. "Okay, Mrs. Sanders, I need to have you scoot as far to your left as possible."

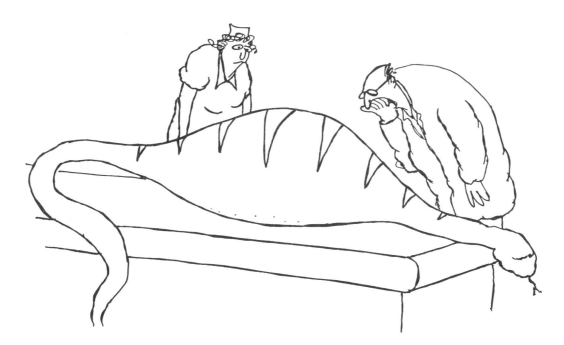

Now, my editor actually came up with the third caption, and we laughed for a good five minutes over it. So I said, "That's perfect! Let's run it." He said, nope, can't deal with snake diarrhea in the newspapers. I said, "Come on! No one's going to see snake diarrhea, it's just kind of inferred." But he felt it was just too gross an image—so he killed even his own caption!

We went with number four, which I also like. But it's hard to top snake diarrhea.

Angry Letters

One thing I've learned as a cartoonist is that no matter how tame a cartoon may seem, someone out there will be offended by it. Having my e-mail address on my cartoons drives this point home even more clearly. What truly amazes me is not so much that people get upset about cartoons, but that they have the time to write to me about it. And the cartoons that set people off are rarely the ones that I'm expecting to get people a bit riled. Understand, I never set out to upset people with my cartoons. I'm trying to entertain people and get them to laugh. But what is funny to one person is an outrage to another. I think all cartoonists have a fantasy of drawing the perfect cartoon that everyone who sees it would agree is very funny. It'll never happen.

So here are some cartoons that really ticked people off and the responses that I got.

Here is a pretty simple, straightforward cartoon. A passenger gets on an airplane and sees that instead of the usual five hundred dials and gauges, this plane just has a big lever that says "Fly" and "Land." What could be upsetting to someone about this?

Dear Mr. McPherson:
I am a pilot for TWA. NEVER in my entire life have I been so offended and disgusted by a cartoon! How dare you insinuate that my job is so mindless as to be performed by the simple switching of a lever. Obviously, you have never seen the inside of an airliner's cockpit. Rather than the simplistic machine you show it to be, an airplane has hundreds of controls that require years of study to master. We pilots' train relentlessly so that people like to you can be carried safely to your destination.

In the future I hope you will pause and reflect before you so thoughtlessly hurt people with your attempt at humor.

Sincerely,
Phil, TWA pilot

You can imagine what I wanted to say to this guy, but I try to wait a day before I respond to a nutty e-mail. I wrote back the next day and told him that yes, I understood that airplanes have hundreds of dials and gauges, but wouldn't it be funny if there was just this one airplane that was controlled by a big lever? I schmoozed a bit about what a great job pilots do and the following day got this response:

Dear John:
I looked at the cartoon again. I can't believe what a jerk I was. Please accept my apologies and keep up the great work.
I was pretty stunned, I have to say. Nice to get a little vindication.

This next cartoon got me more outraged e-mails than any I have ever done. It's really kind of a weird cartoon. Sometimes I'm not even sure what I was trying to say with it, but man, did ferret owners get ticked. Here is one of over three hundred angry e-mails that I got after this appeared.

Dear Mr. McPherson:
Today's cartoon is a vile and heinous depiction of ferrets! Ferrets are warm and loving creatures who would never harm a soul. Your cartoon cruelly perpetuates a stereotype of ferrets as being vicious animals.
SHAME ON YOU!
Disgustedly,
A reader in Worcerster, Massachussetts

Now, honestly, I knew nothing about ferrets at the time. I didn't know if they bit people or not. I just kind of liked the phrase "leaping ferrets." But apparently, it's a pretty sensitive topic. I remember some of the e-mails said, "Die, ferret-hating scum!!" After I'd gotten about one hundred or so angry e-mails, I got the following email:

Dear Mr. McPherson:
Today's cartoon about the ferrets was fantastic! We used to own two ferrets but we had to get rid of them because they constantly bit the snot out of our noses! Thanks for showing what ferrets are truly like.
Sincerely,
A reader in Ohio

Now I realized there were two sides to the ferret debate. And as more angry e-mails poured in about how cuddly and nice ferrets are, I would just forward this guy's e-mail on to them. Along with the 350 or more angry e-mails, I also received about 250 e-mails telling stories about ferrets biting their owners.

I really don't know what ferrets are like and wasn't trying to ferret-bash. I've often done cartoons about toddlers who throw tantrums, so am I saying that all little kids are raging monsters? Of course not. Likewise, I wasn't inferring that all ferrets bite. It's just pretty amazing how many ferret owners got their hackles up over this.

I do cartoons on all kinds of medicine, and rarely if ever do I get an upset letter from medical people—except for chiropractors. I guess for some reason they are sensitive about the legitimacy of their work (Hey, I go to a chiropractor!) so when a cartoon appears, some of them feel they are being mocked, which they are. But then again, I mock everyone and try to be an equal-opportunity mocker. I'm just trying to get people to laugh, not make sweeping statements about someone or some profession, except chiropractors. (I'M KIDDING! I'M KIDDING!).

Anyway, several chiropractors were upset by this cartoon, but I thought this e-mail was the best of them.

Dear Sir:
While I understand your intent at humor regarding this cartoon, we in the chiropractic field have worked long and hard to educate the public about the benefits of properly applied spinal manipulative therapy and dispel scary myths and stereotypes. One little cartoon in a syndicated feature like yours does more to undermine our efforts than you can imagine!

On the day that this cartoon appeared in our local paper, a seventy-six-year-old female patient failed to show up for her weekly appointment. We called her home and grew concerned when she did not answer. About an hour later, one of my staff members found her in our hallway. She was sobbing and held up a copy of your cartoon, and said she was not going to come for her appointment because she did not want THIS to happen to her. It took my staff and me forty-five minutes to calm her and convince her that I was not going to jump off a stepladder onto her back . . .

He continued with more rhetoric, but that was the meat of the letter.

Here was my response:

Dear Dr. Miller (the name has been changed to protect the nutty):
Do you honestly expect me to believe that because of my cartoon, readers across America now think that chiropractors routinely jump off stepladders as part of their treatment? If that's the case, you have not done nearly the job of educating the public that you think you have.
Regards,
John McPherson

He actually wrote back a few days later to tell me that seven more patients had fearfully brought in my cartoon and were afraid to receive treatment. What could I even say to that? There are some real nuts out there.

Meanwhile, I received scores of e-mails from other chiropractors telling me how much they liked the cartoon.

What could be upsetting about this cartoon? Read on.

Dear Mr. McPherson:
Bathroom humor is NOT acceptable in a family newspaper! I do not choose to have such in my paper!
CLEAN UP YOUR ACT!
Disgustedly,
A reader in Washington, D.C.

This woman was upset not by the snake coming out of the toilet, but by the fact that there was a drawing of a toilet in the cartoon. When you consider the fact that most papers only run Close to Home about three inches high, she was offended by a ¼-inch drawing of a toilet. Which makes me wonder what seeing a real toilet up close must do to her. I considered this one too nutty to even respond to.

In addition to upset letters, I do get some really cool letters as well. It's always fun to get feed-back from people all over the world and know that people are out there tuning in.

This cartoon got a lot of very favorable responses. A lot of people who had angioplasty wrote to tell me how much they appreciated the humor. But one man in particular made my day. He wrote to tell me that on the day that this cartoon appeared in his paper, he was scheduled for angioplasty following a heart attack. When the surgical team saw the cartoon in the paper that day, they took the cartoon, blew it up to poster size, and plastered it all over the operating room. When he was wheeled in for the surgery, he saw the cartoon and started laughing and everyone in the OR broke out laughing as well. He wanted me to know how the cartoon helped defuse the tension of the moment and helped get him through a harrowing time in his life.

Soon after this cartoon ran, I got a letter from the public information office at the Supreme Court, saying they loved this cartoon and asked if it would be possible to get the original. So, of course I whisked it over to them.

The day after this cartoon ran, I got a call from Disney saying that an anonymous buyer wished to purchase the cartoon. I said, anonymous, eh? They refused to reveal who the buyer was. So, I sold it to them, and then a few weeks later got a very nice letter from Michael Eisner, thanking me for featuring him in a cartoon and for the original. Very cool of him, I thought.

Close to Home creator John McPherson (center) with *For Better or For Worse* creator Lynn Johnston (left), and *FoxTrot* creator Bill Amend (right).

About the Author

John McPherson is a cartoonist, author, and nationally known speaker on the topic of humor, stress, and creativity. His nationally syndicated cartoon panel, *Close To Home*, appears in over 700 papers worldwide, among them the *Washington Post,* the *Miami Herald,* the *Tokyo Times,* and the *Denver Post.* He has published over 25 collections of his cartoons, various greeting cards, and a yearly day-to-day calendar through Andrews McMeel Publishing. He lives in Saratoga Springs, New York.

Andrews McMeel Publishing
a division of Andrews McMeel Universal
1130 Walnut Street, Kansas City, Missouri 64106

24 25 26 27 28 SDB 10 9 8 7 6 5 4 3 2 1

ISBN: 978-1-4494-8933-5

Library of Congress Control Number: 2017936179

Cover design by Griffin McPherson

www.andrewsmcmeel.com

www.closetohome.com

ATTENTION: SCHOOLS AND BUSINESSES

Andrews McMeel books are available at quantity discounts with bulk purchase for educational, business, or sales promotional use. For information, please e-mail the Andrews McMeel Publishing Special Sales Department:
sales@amuniversal.com.